U.S. SYMBOLS
UNCLE SAM

by Tyler Monroe

Consulting Editor: Gail Saunders-Smith, PhD

CAPSTONE PRESS
a capstone imprint

Pebble Plus is published by Capstone Press,
1710 Roe Crest Drive, North Mankato, Minnesota 56003
www.capstonepub.com

Library of Congress Cataloging-in-Publication Data
Monroe, Tyler, 1976–
  Uncle Sam / by Tyler Monroe.
      pages cm.—(Pebble plus. U.S. symbols)
  Includes bibliographical references and index.
  Summary: "Simple text and full-color photographs briefly describe the iconic Uncle Sam image and its role as a national symbol"—Provided by publisher.
  ISBN 978-1-4765-3086-4 (library binding)—ISBN 978-1-4765-3508-1 (ebook pdf)— ISBN 978-1-4765-3535-7 (pbk.)
1. Uncle Sam (Symbolic character)—Juvenile literature. 2. Wilson, Samuel, 1766–1854—Juvenile literature. 3. United States—Biography—Juvenile literature. I. Title.
  E179.M77 2014
  398.20973'02—dc23
  [B]   2013001827

Editorial Credits
Erika L. Shores, editor; Lori Bye, designer; Svetlana Zhurkin, media researcher; Eric Manske, production specialist

Photo Credits
Alamy: Ian Shaw, 19, North Wind Picture Archives, 9; BigStockPhoto: Cacci, 7, Texas Chick, 21; Corbis: Bettmann, 13, 15; iStockphotos: Todd Keith, 5; Library of Congress, cover, 16, 17; Shutterstock: Morgan Lane Photography, 1, Suat Gursozlu (stars), cover and throughout; Wikipedia: Daderot, 11

Note to Parents and Teachers

The U.S. Symbols set supports national social studies standards related to people, places, and culture. This book describes and illustrates Uncle Sam as a symbol of the United States. The images support early readers in understanding the text. The repetition of words and phrases helps early readers learn new words. This book also introduces early readers to subject-specific vocabulary words, which are defined in the Glossary section. Early readers may need assistance to read some words and to use the Table of Contents, Glossary, Read More, Internet Sites, and Index sections of the book.

Printed in China by Nordica.
0314/CA21400181
022014   007226NORDF13

TABLE OF CONTENTS

Uncle Sam

Uncle Sam is a symbol

of the U.S. government.

People dress up like Uncle Sam

and draw pictures of him.

Uncle Sam has a white beard
and a top hat. He wears a blue
coat and striped pants. Many people
think Uncle Sam was based on
a man named Samuel Wilson.

During the War of 1812,

Wilson packed meat in barrels.

The U.S. government then stamped

"U.S." on the barrels. The barrels

of meat were sent to soldiers.

Some soldiers thought "U.S."

stood for Wilson, or "Uncle Sam."

People began calling anything

from the government "Uncle Sam's."

A statue of Samuel Wilson stands in Arlington, Massachusetts.

A Government Symbol

Newspapers often used cartoons to show world events. Artists began drawing pictures of Uncle Sam. He stood for the U.S. government in the cartoons.

In 1876 the United States turned 100 years old. People sold gifts of all kinds to celebrate. Many items had pictures of Uncle Sam on them.

1776

1870

PACIFIC OCEAN

ATLANTIC OCEAN

15

James Montgomery Flagg painted

the most famous picture

of Uncle Sam in 1916.

It was used on a poster asking

men to join the U.S. Army.

17

President George H. W. Bush
made an official Uncle Sam Day
in 1989. It was on September 13,
Samuel Wilson's birthday.

The Symbol Today

Uncle Sam is an important U.S. symbol today. He reminds Americans to be proud of their country.

Glossary

celebrate—to do something fun on a special day

government—the group of people who make laws, rules, and decisions for a country or state

soldier—a person who is in the military

symbol—an object that stands for something else

War of 1812—a war between the United States and Great Britain; it lasted from 1812 to 1815

Read More

Hewitt, David. *Uncle Sam's America: A Parade through Our Star-Spangled History.* New York: Simon & Schuster Books for Young Readers, 2008.

Kishel, Ann-Marie. *U.S. Symbols.* First Step Nonfiction. Minneapolis: Lerner Publications Company, 2007.

Suen, Anastasia. *Uncle Sam.* American Symbols. Minneapolis: Picture Window Books, 2009.

Internet Sites

FactHound offers a safe, fun way to find Internet sites related to this book. All of the sites on FactHound have been researched by our staff.

Here's all you do:

Visit *www.facthound.com*

Type in this code: 9781476530864

Super-cool stuff! Check out projects, games and lots more at www.capstonekids.com

Critical Thinking Using the Common Core

1. Look at the photograph on page 7. Describe Uncle Sam's clothing and why it reminds people of the United States. (Integration of Knowledge and Ideas)

2. Look at the cartoon on page 13. What do you think is the illustrator's opinion of the U.S. government in this cartoon? Why? (Integration of Knowledge and Ideas)

3. What made James Montgomery Flagg's painting of Uncle Sam a good poster for the U.S. Army? (Key Ideas and Details)

Index

Word Count: 211
Grade: 1
Early-Intervention Level: 22